A KITCHEN IN ALGERIA

CLASSICAL AND CONTEMPORARY ALGERIAN RECIPES

By
Umm Maryam

Published by
BookSumo, a division of Saxonberg Associates
http://www.booksumo.com/

INTRODUCTION

Hello, my friend. I would like to thank you personally for taking the time to purchase my book: *A Kitchen in Algeria: Classical and Contemporary Algerian Recipes.* I truly do hope that these recipes are reaching you in the best of health and a period of happiness.

In writing this book I have taken the time to compile, what I believe to be, the simplest and easiest, classical Turkish dishes into one source for those of my readers who are cultural food lovers.

After publishing my first book: *Arabia & Asia: A Cookbook with Recipes from Egypt, Morocco, Persia, & Pakistan* I noticed a strong interest in this type of food. So I made the decision to continue this cooking journey by focusing on a new country.

If you are interested in my first cookbook then please see the last few pages of this book where I've provided a link for where to find my seminal cookbook.

If you are interested in any specific type of food then please let me know. I'm very easy to find

:)

In writing this book, I have tried to improve the style and content since my last cookbook. For each recipe, you will read I've taken the care to provide not only ingredients with specific directions.

But I've also tried to provide accurate information on the amount of time it will take to prepare and cook each dish, so you can plan accordingly before embarking on a specific cooking journey. Each recipe also contains information on its nutritional value as well as serving information. So for my health conscience readers check the caloric and fat contents of each dish.

I really want to provide the most value for you, my readers, so I figured this information will help a bit more. I'm constantly trying to improve and I listen to my readers. So please help me with feedback!

You'll find that many of the recipes require a lot of spice so make sure you have a lot of the following ingredients: coriander, cumin, yogurt, salt, pepper, cayenne, fresh garlic and onions, turmeric, and curry.

So without further ado, I will stop talking. Let's get our frying pans and food processors ready and take a trip to Algeria with some simple and easy recipes!

TABLE OF CONTENTS

Any Issues? Contact Me

If you find that something important to you is missing from this book please contact me at umm@booksumo.com.

I will try my best to re-publish a revised copy taking your feedback into consideration and let you know when the book has been revised with you in mind.

:)

— Umm Maryam

Legal Notes

COMMON ABBREVIATIONS

cup(s)	C.
tablespoon	tbsp
teaspoon	tsp
ounce	oz
pound	lb

*All units used are standard American measurements

CHAPTER 1: CLASSICAL AND CONTEMPORARY ALGERIAN RECIPES

BEEF & HOMINY STEW

Ingredients

- 1 lb lean ground beef
- 1 1/2 C. onions, chopped
- 1 C. green bell pepper, chopped
- 3 garlic cloves, crushed
- 8 oz. canned kidney beans
- 8 oz. hominy
- 1 tsp salt
- 1 tsp dried basil
- 1/2 tsp ground black pepper
- 1/4 tsp sugar
- 1/4 tsp dried oregano
- 1/4 tsp red pepper flakes
- 2 C. water

Directions

- In a large skillet, add the beef, bell pepper, onion and garlic on medium heat and cook for about 6 minutes.
- Drain the excess fat and stir in the remaining ingredients and bring to a gentle boil.
- Simmer for about 10 minutes till desired consistency.
- This stew is great when served with pasta or rice.

Amount per serving: 6

Timing Information:

Preparation	12 mins
Total Time	28 mins

Nutritional Information:

Calories	217.0
Fat	8.2g
Cholesterol	49.1mg
Sodium	633.8mg
Carbohydrates	16.6g
Protein	18.4g

* Percent Daily Values are based on a 2,000 calorie diet.

CHICKPEA & EGG PIE

Ingredients

- 2 C. chickpea flour
- 4 C. water
- 1/2 C. canola oil
- 1 tbsp salt
- 1/4 tsp black pepper
- 1 egg, beaten
- ground cumin, for sprinkling
- harissa

Directions

- Set your oven to 350 degrees F before doing anything else.
- In a food processor, add the flour, salt, oil and water and pulse till smooth.
- Transfer the mixture into a 10x6-inch metal pan and top with beaten egg evenly.
- Cook in the oven for about 1 hour.
- Remove from the oven and sprinkle with the cumin.
- Cut the pie into slices and serve with harissa.

Amount per serving: 10

Timing Information:

Preparation	5 mins
Total Time	1 hr 5 mins

Nutritional Information:

Calories	174.8
Fat	12.6g
Cholesterol	18.6mg
Sodium	719.3mg
Carbohydrates	10.7g
Protein	4.7g

* Percent Daily Values are based on a 2,000 calorie diet.

VEGGIE STEW WITH COUSCOUS

Ingredients

- 1 large onion, chopped
- 1/2 tsp turmeric
- 1/4 tsp cayenne
- 1/2 C. vegetable stock
- 1/2 tbsp cinnamon
- 1 1/2 tsps black pepper
- 1/2 tsp salt
- 5 tbsps tomato puree

- 3-4 whole cloves
- 3 medium zucchini
- 4 small yellow squash
- 3/4 large carrot
- 4 medium yellow potatoes, skins on
- 1 red bell pepper
- 1 (15 oz.) can garbanzo beans

Directions

- In a large pan, heat the broth on medium-low heat and sauté the onion till soft.
- Stir in the spices and sauté for a few minutes more.
- Stir in the tomato paste and cook for about 2 minutes.
- Meanwhile cut the vegetables into large chunks.
- In the pan, add all the vegetables, a pinch of cinnamon and enough water to cover the mixture and bring to a boil.
- Reduce the heat and simmer covered for about 1-2 hours till desired doneness.

- Stir in the beans and simmer for about 5 minutes.
- Serve this veggie stew over the couscous.

Amount per serving: 4

Timing Information:

Preparation	15 mins
Total Time	1 hr 35 mins

Nutritional Information:

Calories	361.6
Fat	2.5g
Cholesterol	0.0mg
Sodium	681.7mg
Carbohydrates	75.6g
Protein	13.3g

* Percent Daily Values are based on a 2,000 calorie diet.

Meat Filled Pastries

(Borek)

Ingredients

- 250 g beef mince
- 1 onion, chopped
- 1 pinch cinnamon
- 1 1/2 C. parsley, finely chopped
- 2 eggs, beaten
- 6 phyllo pastry sheets
- 6 Laughing Cow cheese
- vegetable oil

Directions

- In a large skillet, heat a little oil and sauté the onion for about 5 minutes.
- Stir in the beef and cook till browned.
- Stir in parsley, pinch of cinnamon, salt and black pepper.
- Gently, stir in beaten eggs, but take care not to scramble the eggs.
- Remove from heat and let it cool.
- Divide the beef mixture over each pastry sheet, about 1 1/2-inch from the bottom and leave about 1-inch from both sides.
- Cut the cheese in half and place over the mixture.
- Fold both sides of the pastry sheet to the middle and roll it.
- Fry the rolls in hot vegetable oil till golden brown.

Amount per serving: 6

Timing Information:

Preparation	1 hr
Total Time	1 hr 5 mins

Nutritional Information:

Calories	175.4
Fat	9.6g
Cholesterol	29.5mg
Sodium	128.8mg
Carbohydrates	12.6g
Protein	9.1g

* Percent Daily Values are based on a 2,000 calorie diet.

North African Style Poached Eggs
(Chakchouka)

Ingredients

- 3 tbsps olive oil
- 1/2 tsp cumin seed
- 1 tbsp paprika
- 1 onion, thinly sliced
- 1 tbsp harissa
- 2 -3 garlic cloves, minced
- 3 tomatoes, peeled, seeded and diced
- 1 potato, small diced cubes
- 1 green bell pepper, diced

- 1 red bell pepper, diced
- 1 yellow bell pepper, diced
- 1-2 chili pepper
- 1 C. water
- kosher salt
- fresh ground pepper
- 4 eggs
- parsley or cilantro, chopped
- black olives
- capers

Directions

- In a large deep skillet, heat the oil on medium heat and sauté cumin seeds for about 15 seconds.
- Stir in the paprika and sauté for about 10-15 seconds.
- Add the garlic and onion and sauté for about 5 minutes.

- Stir in the tomatoes and bring to a simmer and stir in the potatoes, peppers, water, salt and black pepper.
- Reduce the heat to low and simmer, covered for at least 10 minutes.
- Make 4 wells in the veggie mixture and carefully, crack 1 egg in each well.
- Simmer, covered for about 10 minutes.
- Serve with a garnishing of olives, capers and parsley.

Amount per serving: 4

Timing Information:

Preparation	10 mins
Total Time	30 mins

Nutritional Information:

Calories	252.8
Fat	15.5g
Cholesterol	186.0mg
Sodium	85.8mg
Carbohydrates	20.5g
Protein	9.4g

* Percent Daily Values are based on a 2,000 calorie diet.

ALGERIAN CUCUMBER SALAD

Ingredients

- 1 large cucumber, peeled, halved lengthwise, seeded, thinly sliced
- 1/2 green capsicum, cored, seeded and cut in half lengthwise
- 1/3 C. pitted and coarsely chopped green olives
- 4 large fresh mint leaves, finely chopped
- 2 tbsps finely chopped fresh coriander leaves
- 1/2 tsp paprika
- 1/4 C. extra virgin olive oil
- 3 1/2 tsps white wine vinegar
- salt & freshly ground black pepper

Directions

- In a large bowl, add all the ingredients and toss to coat well and serve immediately.

Amount per serving: 2

Timing Information:

Preparation	15 mins
Total Time	15 mins

Nutritional Information:

Calories	301.6
Fat	30.7g
Cholesterol	0.0mg
Sodium	353.5mg
Carbohydrates	8.0g
Protein	1.5g

* Percent Daily Values are based on a 2,000 calorie diet.

LEMONY SEMOLINA CAKE

Ingredients

For the cake:

- 1 1/2 C. of coarse semolina
- 1 C. plain flour
- 2 tsps baking powder
- 3/4 C. unsweetened dried shredded coconut
- 1/4 C. granulated sugar
- 1 C. sunflower oil
- 1 lemon, zest of, finely grated
- 1 C. yogurt
- 4 eggs
- 2 tsps vanilla flavoring

For the Syrup

- 3 C. water
- 3 C. granulated sugar
- 1 tbsp orange flower water
- 1 tsp lemon juice
- To Decorate
- blanched whole almond

Directions

- Set your oven to 355 degrees F before doing anything else and grease an 11x7-inch baking dish.
- For the Syrup, in a pan, add the water and sugar and bring to a boil and simmer till pale golden syrup forms.
- Remove from heat and immediately, stir in the orange flower water and lemon juice and keep aside to cool.

- In a large bowl, mix together the flour, semolina, granulated sugar, baking powder and coconut.
- In another bowl, add the remaining ingredients and beat till smooth and creamy.
- Add the egg mixture into the flour mixture and mix till well combined.
- Transfer the mixture into the prepared baking dish evenly and with the back of a spatula, smooth the surface.
- With a knife, make diamond pattern on top and insert 1 almond in each pattern.
- Cook in the oven for about 30-40 minutes.
- Remove the cake from the oven and cut through the pattern.
- Place the syrup over the cake evenly and keep aside for about 2 hours.

Amount per serving: 1

Timing Information:

Preparation	10 mins
Total Time	50 mins

Nutritional Information:

Calories	6699.1
Fat	290.2g4
Cholesterol	775.8mg2
Sodium	1180.8mg
Carbohydrates	963.8g3
Protein	83.3g

* Percent Daily Values are based on a 2,000 calorie diet.

SPICED GREEN BEANS

Ingredients

- 1 lb fresh green beans
- 2 tbsps grapeseed oil
- 1 garlic clove, finely minced
- 1/2 tsp ground cumin
- 1/4 tsp paprika
- 1/4 tsp ground cloves
- 1 tbsp slivered almonds

Directions

- Rinse and trim the green beans and cook in a pan of salted boiling water for about 1 minute.
- Drain and rinse under cold water and transfer into a bowl.
- In a skillet, heat oil on medium heat and sauté all the remaining ingredients for about 2 minutes.
- Add the garlic mixture into the bowl with the green beans and toss to coat well and serve warm.

Amount per serving: 4

Timing Information:

Preparation	10 mins
Total Time	15 mins

Nutritional Information:

Calories	107.9
Fat	7.9g
Cholesterol	0.0mg
Sodium	7.8mg
Carbohydrates	8.8g
Protein	2.5g

* Percent Daily Values are based on a 2,000 calorie diet.

Jam Sandwich Cookies

Ingredients

For the Sables

- 1 C. butter, softened
- 1/2 C. granulated sugar
- 1 large free range egg
- 2 1/2 C. all-purpose flour
- 1/2 tsp vanilla extract
- To decorate
- 3/4 C. strawberry jam
- 1/2-3/4 C. icing sugar

Directions

- Set your oven to 340 degrees F before doing anything else and line a baking tray with foil, shiny side up.
- In a bowl, add the sugar and margarine and beat till fluffy.
- Add the egg and vanilla extract and beat till well combined.
- Slowly, add the flour and baking powder and mix till a soft dough forms.
- On a floured surface with a rolling pin, roll the dough to 1/4-inch thickness.
- Cut the tops and bottoms from the dough and place onto prepared baking tray in a single layer.

- Cook in the oven for about 8 minutes.
- Remove from the oven and keep aside to cool completely.
- In a pan, add jam and heat till bubbling.
- Remove from heat and let it cool slightly.
- In a large tray, arrange the top of the cookies and sprinkle with icing sugar.
- Place about 1/2 tsp of jam over the underside of the bottom cookies.
- Carefully, arrange the top cookies over the jam.
- Keep aside to set completely before serving.

Amount per serving: 1

Timing Information:

Preparation	25 mins
Total Time	33 mins

Nutritional Information:

Calories	142.4
Fat	3.9g
Cholesterol	7.4mg
Sodium	64.5mg
Carbohydrates	25.1g
Protein	1.6g

* Percent Daily Values are based on a 2,000 calorie diet.

ALMOND BALLS

Ingredients

- 3 C. ground almonds
- 1 C. granulated sugar
- 3 small eggs
- 1 1/2 tsps baking powder
- 1/2 tsp vanilla extract
- 1/2 C. chopped almonds
- glace cherries, to decorate

Directions

- Set your oven to 340 degrees F before doing anything else and grease and flour a baking sheet.
- In a large bowl, add ground almonds, sugar, vanilla and baking powder and mix till well combined.
- Add eggs, one at a time and mix till a firm paste forms.
- Make small equal sized ball from the mixture.
- In a shallow dish, place chopped almonds.
- Roll the balls into chopped almonds evenly and arrange onto prepared baking sheet in a single layer.

- Gently, press 1/4 of a cherry in the center of each ball and cook in the oven for about 12 minutes.

Amount per serving: 1

Timing Information:

| Preparation | 15 mins |
| Total Time | 27 mins |

Nutritional Information:

Calories	95.1
Fat	5.9g
Cholesterol	15.6mg
Sodium	23.4mg
Carbohydrates	8.9g
Protein	2.8g

* Percent Daily Values are based on a 2,000 calorie diet.

CARROTS IN HOT SAUCE

Ingredients

- 500 g carrots
- 3 tbsps olive oil
- 3 garlic cloves, minced
- 1 hot pepper
- 1/2 tsp caraway seed
- 1 tsp paprika
- 1 1/2 tbsps vinegar
- salt and black pepper

Directions

- Peel the carrots and then slice into rounds.
- Cook the carrot in lightly salted water till tender enough.
- Meanwhile for sauce in a grinder, add the garlic, caraway seeds, hot pepper and paprika and some salt and grind till a paste forms.
- Transfer the sauce into a bowl and add the oil and 1 tbsp of water and mix till well combined.
- Drain the carrots and return to the pan with sauce on low heat.
- Cook, covered till the carrots absorb the flavor of the sauce.
- Stir in vinegar and serve hot.

Amount per serving: 4

Timing Information:

Preparation	10 mins
Total Time	40 mins

Nutritional Information:

Calories	148.2
Fat	10.6g
Cholesterol	0.0mg
Sodium	87.1mg
Carbohydrates	13.1g
Protein	1.4g

* Percent Daily Values are based on a 2,000 calorie diet.

Sesame Seeds Farina Rolls

Ingredients

- 1/4 oz. active dry yeast
- 1/4 C. warm water, lightly salted
- 1 1/2 tbsps olive oil
- 1 C. farina (cream of wheat)
- 3/4 C. whole wheat flour
- 1/2 tsp salt
- 1/2 C. water
- 2 tbsps sesame seeds, toasted
- 1 egg, beaten
- cooking spray

Directions

- In a bowl, mix together 1/4 C. of salted water and yeast and keep aside for at least 5 minutes.
- In a large bowl, mix together farina, flour and salt and then add in olive oil.
- Add the yeast mixture and stir to combine well.
- Slowly, add 1/2 C. of water, stirring continuously till well a smooth dough forms.

- With a damp cloth, cover the dough and keep it in warm place for about 1 1/2 hours.
- Set your oven to 400 degrees F and grease a baking sheet.
- Just 2 minutes before baking, mix the sesame seeds into the dough.
- Divide the dough into 15 equal sized balls and arrange onto the prepared baking sheet in a single layer.
- Coat each ball with the beaten egg and cook in the oven for about 20 minutes.

Amount per serving: 1

Timing Information:

Preparation	1 hr 40 mins
Total Time	2 hrs

Nutritional Information:

Calories	88.7
Fat	2.4g
Cholesterol	14.1mg
Sodium	83.4mg
Carbohydrates	13.9g
Protein	2.8g

* Percent Daily Values are based on a 2,000 calorie diet.

CHICKPEAS SOUFFLÉ SANDWICH

Ingredients

For soufflé:

- 2 C. chickpea flour
- 4 C. water
- 1/2 C. sunflower oil
- 2 -3 tsps salt
- 1/4 tsp black pepper
- 1 egg, beaten

- 1 1/2-2 tsps cumin

To serve:

- 4 tbsps harissa
- 2 large French baguettes
- 1 tbsp cumin

Directions

- Set your oven to 355 degrees F before doing anything else.
- For soufflé, in a large blender, add all the ingredients except eggs and pulse till smooth and frothy.
- Transfer the mixture in an 11x7-inch pyrex dish evenly.
- Place the beaten egg over the mixture evenly and cook in the oven for about 45 minutes.
- Remove from the oven and cut into 8 slices.
- Cut the each baguette in 4 pieces and then split them open.
- Carefully discard some of the inner bread and arrange the outside shells on a smooth surface.

- Place about 1/2 tbsp of harissa over the bottom of baguette piece, followed by soufflé slice.
- Sprinkle with cumin and make a sandwich by covering with the top baguette.

Amount per serving: 8

Timing Information:

Preparation	5 mins
Total Time	50 mins

Nutritional Information:

Calories	292.2
Fat	16.4g
Cholesterol	23.2mg
Sodium	733.5mg
Carbohydrates	27.4g
Protein	8.9g

* Percent Daily Values are based on a 2,000 calorie diet.

CHICKEN & VEGGIE STEW

Ingredients

- 3 C. chicken broth
- 1 chicken bouillon cube
- 2 C. cooked chicken, chopped
- 1 medium onion, chopped
- 2 C. fresh green beans, cut
- 2 carrots, sliced
- 1 tsp ground cumin
- 1 tsp basil
- 1 garlic clove, minced
- 2 bay leaves
- 1/2 tsp dried parsley
- salt
- pepper
- 2 medium tomatoes, chopped
- 2 small zucchini, sliced
- 1 (16 oz.) can garbanzo beans, drained
- 1/4 tsp ground red pepper

Directions

- In a large pan, add the chicken, carrots, green beans, onion, garlic, parsley, basil, cumin, bay leaves, salt, black pepper, bouillon cube and broth and bring to a boil.
- Reduce the heat and simmer, covered for about 8 minutes.
- Stir in the zucchini and tomatoes and cook for some time.
- Stir in the beans and red pepper and cook till heated completely.
- This stew will be great over a bowl of hot couscous.

Amount per serving: 6

Timing Information:

Preparation	15 mins
Total Time	40 mins

Nutritional Information:

Calories	230.8
Fat	5.1g
Cholesterol	35.0mg
Sodium	816.1mg
Carbohydrates	26.6g
Protein	19.9g

* Percent Daily Values are based on a 2,000 calorie diet.

SEMOLINA WITH HONEY

Ingredients

- 1 C. of ground semolina
- 3 tbsps unsalted butter
- 2 tbsps of natural set honey
- ground cinnamon
- silver dragees
- paper tea roses

Directions

- In a pan, add the semolina on medium-high heat and cook, shaking the pan till toasted completely.
- Transfer into a bowl and keep aside.
- In the same pan, melt the butter and remove from heat and immediately stir the honey to combine well.
- Place the semolina in the pan and stir to combine.
- Transfer the Semolina mixture into a serving plate and sprinkle with cinnamon.
- Serve with a garnishing of paper tea roses and silver dredges.

Amount per serving: 4

Timing Information:

Preparation	5 mins
Total Time	10 mins

Nutritional Information:

Calories	258.5
Fat	9.0g
Cholesterol	22.9mg
Sodium	2.0mg
Carbohydrates	39.0g
Protein	5.4g

* Percent Daily Values are based on a 2,000 calorie diet.

Sweet & Spicy Carrots

Ingredients

- 2 1/2 lbs carrots, peeled and sliced
- 1/2 tsp hot sauce
- 2 tbsps light olive oil
- 3 garlic cloves, sliced thinly
- 1 lemon, juice of
- 2 tsps cumin seeds
- 1/2 tsp sugar
- 1/2 tsp salt
- 2 tbsps mint, finely chopped

Directions

- In a steamer basket, steam the carrots for about 5 minutes.
- Drain well, reserving about 5 tbsps of the cooking liquid.
- Meanwhile heat a dry skillet and toast the cumin seeds till fragrant.
- In a large pan, heat the oil and sauté the garlic for about 1 minute.
- Stir in carrots, sugar, cumin seeds, salt, lemon juice, hot sauce and reserved cooking liquid on medium-low heat.
- Cover partially and simmer for about 10 minutes.
- Stir in the mint and serve immediately.

Amount per serving: 4

Timing Information:

Preparation	5 mins
Total Time	20 mins

Nutritional Information:

Calories	189.8
Fat	7.7g
Cholesterol	0.0mg
Sodium	505.7mg
Carbohydrates	30.2g
Protein	3.1g

* Percent Daily Values are based on a 2,000 calorie diet.

LEMONY COOKIES

Ingredients

- 1 kg plain flour
- 6 eggs
- 250 g granulated sugar
- 2 tsps baking powder
- 1/4 liter sunflower oil
- Lemon Version
- 4 lemons, zest of, finely grated

Directions

- Line a cookie sheet with aluminum foil.
- In a large bowl, add the oil and 6 eggs and beat well.
- Add the lemon zest and baking powder and mix well.
- Slowly, add the flour, beating continuously till a dough forms.
- Place the dough onto a lightly floured surface and roll to 0.20-inch thickness.
- With a cookie cutter, cut the desired size cookies and coat the top with the beaten egg.
- Arrange the cookies onto prepared cookie sheet in a single layer.
- Cook in the oven for about 25-28 minutes.

Amount per serving: 1

Timing Information:

Preparation	30 mins
Total Time	58 mins

Nutritional Information:

Calories	105.1
Fat	4.1g
Cholesterol	18.6mg
Sodium	17.8mg
Carbohydrates	14.6g
Protein	2.2g

* Percent Daily Values are based on a 2,000 calorie diet.

Mini Almond Treat in Sugar Syrup

Ingredients

- 3 C. ground almonds
- 1 C. granulated sugar
- 4 limes, zest of, finely grated
- 3 small medium eggs
- 3 tbsps cornflour
- To decorate
- 2 C. of light sugar syrup
- 2 1/2 C. icing sugar

Directions

- Set your oven to 340 degrees F before doing anything else and arrange the rack in the middle shelf of the oven.
- In a large bowl, add sugar, almonds, eggs and lime zest and mix till a soft dough forms.
- Dust a smooth surface with corn flour.
- Divide the dough into 4 portions and roll on a floured surface into a sausage shape.
- Cut the each sausage into 1 1/4-inch diamond shape pieces.
- Cook in the oven till set and pale in color.

- Meanwhile for sugar syrup, in a pan, cook 1 C. of sugar, 2 C. of water and half of a lime for about 10 minutes.
- Remove from heat and cool slightly.
- In a shallow dish, place icing sugar.
- Remove the cookies from the oven and let them cool slightly.
- Dip the each diamond, one by one in the syrup and hold with a fork to discard excess syrup.
- Then roll the diamond in icing sugar and keep aside.
- After 5 minutes again roll everything in icing sugar.

Amount per serving: 1

Timing Information:

Preparation	30 mins
Total Time	50 mins

Nutritional Information:

Calories	127.4
Fat	5.0g
Cholesterol	14.1mg
Sodium	5.7mg
Carbohydrates	19.2g
Protein	2.5g

* Percent Daily Values are based on a 2,000 calorie diet.

LEMONY ROASTED CHICKEN

Ingredients

- 1 (3-4 lb) roasting chicken
- 2 lemons, halved
- 2 large garlic cloves, minced
- 3 tbsps unsalted butter
- 1 tbsp seasoning, mixed
- 1 1/2 tbsps coarse salt
- coarse salt
- fresh ground pepper
- olive oil
- 3-4 sprigs thyme

Directions

- Set your oven to 450 degrees F before doing anything else and arrange a rack in a roasting pan.
- In a mortar with pestle, mash the garlic with salt.
- In a bowl, mix together the garlic paste, butter and spices.
- With your fingers, loosen the skin under the breast and thighs.
- With your fingers rub the butter mixture under the skin evenly and drizzle with the lemon juice.

- Sprinkle the cavity and outer skin of the chicken with salt and black pepper.
- Stuff the cavity of the chicken with thyme sprigs and 4 lemon halves.
- Arrange the chicken into prepared roasting pan, breast side down.
- Cook in the oven for about 15 minutes.
- Remove the roasting pan from the oven and place the chicken breast side up.
- Now, reduce the temperature of oven to 350 degrees F.
- Cook in the oven for about 90 minutes, basting with water and olive oil occasionally.
- If chicken becomes brown too soon then cover with a foil for about 60-75 minutes and then remove before last 15 minutes of cooking.

Amount per serving: 4

Timing Information:

| Preparation | 20 mins |
| Total Time | 2 hrs |

Nutritional Information:

Calories	562.1
Fat	43.5g
Cholesterol	183.3mg
Sodium	2767.6mg
Carbohydrates	3.3g
Protein	38.1g

* Percent Daily Values are based on a 2,000 calorie diet.

Cheesy Beef & Potato Casserole

Ingredients

- 1 lb potato, peeled, boiled until tender
- 2 tbsps butter
- 1 tsp salt
- 2 tsps olive oil
- 1 small onion, finely chopped
- 1/2 lb ground beef
- 1/4 tsp pepper
- 1 medium egg, beaten
- 2 oz. gruyere cheese, grated

Directions

- Set your oven to 350 degrees F before doing anything else and grease a casserole dish.
- In a bowl, add the boiled potatoes, butter and salt and mash completely.
- Heat a skillet and stir fry the beef, onion and pepper for about 5 minutes.
- Drain the excess liquid and fat from the beef mixture.
- Place the half of the potato mixture in the bottom of prepared casserole dish evenly.

- Place the beef mixture and then topped with the remaining potato mixture evenly.
- With the back of a spatula, smooth the surface of the potato mixture.
- Brush the top of the potato mixture with the beaten egg and sprinkle with the cheese evenly.
- Cook in the oven for about 30 minutes.

Amount per serving: 6

Timing Information:

Preparation	20 mins
Total Time	50 mins

Nutritional Information:

Calories	241.6
Fat	14.8g
Cholesterol	77.3mg
Sodium	486.7mg
Carbohydrates	14.5g
Protein	12.4g

* Percent Daily Values are based on a 2,000 calorie diet.

ALMOND PASTE DATES

Ingredients

- 24 dates
- 2 drops green food coloring
- 2/3 C. marzipan (almond paste)
- 2 tsps powdered sugar

Directions

- Remove the pit of each date by cutting it lengthwise.
- In a bowl, add the almond paste and food coloring and stir to combine.
- Stuff the dates with the almond paste mixture.
- Serve with a sprinkling of the powdered sugar.

Amount per serving: 1

Timing Information:

Preparation	15 mins
Total Time	15 mins

Nutritional Information:

Calories	20.8
Fat	0.0g
Cholesterol	0.0mg
Sodium	0.1mg
Carbohydrates	5.5g
Protein	0.1g

* Percent Daily Values are based on a 2,000 calorie diet.

Sweet & Sour Lamb with Pear

Ingredients

- 2 1/2 lbs lamb, cubed
- 3 tbsps butter
- 1/2 tsp ground cinnamon
- 3 C. water
- 1/4 C. sugar
- 16 prunes, soaked and drained
- 2 tbsps raisins
- 2 tbsps almonds
- 1 pear, peeled and cubed
- 1/4 C. orange juice
- 1 tsp orange blossom water (mazhar)

Directions

- In a heavy-bottomed pan, melt the butter on low heat and stir fry the lamb for about 5 minutes.
- Stir in the sugar, cinnamon and water and increase the heat to medium.
- Simmer for about 40 minutes.
- Stir in the remaining ingredients except the orange juice and simmer for about 15 minutes more.
- Stir in the orange juice and serve immediately.

Amount per serving: 8

Timing Information:

Preparation	10 mins
Total Time	1 hr 10 mins

Nutritional Information:

Calories	350.0
Fat	19.6g
Cholesterol	86.4mg
Sodium	96.6mg
Carbohydrates	23.4g
Protein	21.0g

* Percent Daily Values are based on a 2,000 calorie diet.

CHICKEN, CHICKPEAS & RICE SOUP

Ingredients

- 4 chicken drumsticks, skinless
- 1 medium brown onion, finely diced
- 200 g canned chick-peas, rinsed & drained
- 2 1/2 liters water
- 2 inches cinnamon sticks
- 1/2 lemon, juice of
- 1 large egg yolk, beaten
- 1/4 C. fresh parsley, finely chopped
- 2 -3 tsps olive oil
- 1 1/2 tbsps basmati rice
- salt & pepper

Directions

- In a large pan, heat the oil and sauté the onion till soft.
- Stir in the chicken and cinnamon sticks and stir fry for about 8 minutes.
- Stir in the salt, black pepper and water and bring to a boil.
- Reduce the heat to medium and simmer, covered for about 75 minutes.
- Remove the chicken from the pan and let it cool slightly.

- Remove the chicken from its bones and add in it to the pan with the chickpeas.
- Simmer, covered for about 15 minutes.
- Stir in the rice and seasoning if required and simmer, covered for about 15 minutes.
- In a bowl, add the egg yolk, lemon juice and a few tsps of the broth and beat well.
- Slowly, add the egg yolk mixture, stirring continuously and simmer for about 1 minute.
- Stir in the parsley and serve hot.

Amount per serving: 6

Timing Information:

Preparation	5 mins
Total Time	2 hrs 5 mins

Nutritional Information:

Calories	160.5
Fat	6.9g
Cholesterol	70.1mg
Sodium	156.4mg
Carbohydrates	12.1g
Protein	12.0g

* Percent Daily Values are based on a 2,000 calorie diet.

Saffron Chicken & Olives Stew

Ingredients

- 2 tbsps olive oil
- 2 lbs boneless skinless chicken breasts, cubed
- 1 tbsp butter
- 4 garlic cloves, minced
- 1 tsp saffron, crumbled
- 1 bunch cilantro, finely chopped
- 1 C. water
- 8 oz. kalamata olives, pitted
- 1 lemon, juiced
- salt & freshly ground black pepper

Directions

- In a large pan, heat the oil and stir fry the chicken for about 10 minutes.
- Stir in the butter, saffron, cilantro and garlic and cook for about 10 minutes.
- Stir in the water and bring to a boil and reduce the heat.
- Simmer for about 25 minutes.
- Stir in the lemon juice and olives and simmer for about 8 minutes more.
- Season with the required amount of the salt and black pepper and remove from heat.
- This stew will be great when served with rice or couscous.

Amount per serving: 4

Timing Information:

Preparation	10 mins
Total Time	1 hr 3 mins

Nutritional Information:

Calories	420.5
Fat	21.7g
Cholesterol	152.9mg
Sodium	715.0mg
Carbohydrates	6.3g
Protein	49.2g

* Percent Daily Values are based on a 2,000 calorie diet.

CHICKEN WITH CHICKPEAS

Ingredients

- 8 chicken legs
- 1 small onion, chopped finely
- 4 garlic cloves, crushed
- 1/2 tsp ras el hanout spice mix
- 1/4 tsp harissa
- 2 allspice berries
- 2 tsps tomato paste
- 400 g chickpeas, drained
- 2 pints chicken stock

Directions

- In a large pan, heat the 2 tbsps of oil and sauté the onion till tender.
- Stir in the chicken and stir fry for about 10 minutes.
- Stir in the tomato puree, garlic, harissa, spices and salt and cook for about 2 minutes.
- Stir in the broth and bring to a boil and simmer for about 30 minutes.
- Stir in the chickpeas and simmer for about 10 minutes.

Amount per serving: 4

Timing Information:

Preparation	5 mins
Total Time	55 mins

Nutritional Information:

Calories	219.0
Fat	4.0g
Cholesterol	7.2mg
Sodium	664.6mg
Carbohydrates	34.2g
Protein	11.5g

* Percent Daily Values are based on a 2,000 calorie diet.

Broad Beans in Spicy Sauce

Ingredients

- 1 kg broad bean, in the pod
- 1 bunch fresh cilantro, chopped
- 6 garlic cloves, minced
- 3-4 tbsps olive oil
- 1 tsp paprika
- 1/4 tsp cayenne
- 1/8 tsp black pepper
- salt, to taste
- 1 -1 1/2 tsps vinegar
- 600 ml water

Directions

- Trim the broad beans and remove the strings but leave the beans in their pod and then cut into 1-inch pieces.
- In a heavy-bottomed pan, sauté the beans and garlic for about 2 minutes.
- Stir in remaining ingredients and simmer, covered for about 25-30 minutes.
- Simmer till desired thickness of sauce.

Amount per serving: 4

Timing Information:

Preparation	5 mins
Total Time	50 mins

Nutritional Information:

Calories	277.7
Fat	10.8g
Cholesterol	0.0mg
Sodium	1140.1mg
Carbohydrates	33.1g
Protein	14.2g

* Percent Daily Values are based on a 2,000 calorie diet.

Pasta with Chicken & Eggs

Ingredients

- 1 whole chicken
- 3/4-1 C. canned chick-peas
- 2 tbsps ghee
- 1/4 tsp black pepper
- 1/2-3/4 tsp cinnamon
- 1 tsp tomato puree, concentrate
- 2 onions, chopped finely
- 1 -2 garlic clove, minced
- 1/2 tsp ras el hanout spice mix
- salt
- 3 -4 eggs
- 500 g orzo pasta
- 1 chicken stock cube
- olive oil

Directions

- In a large pan, melt the ghee and stir fry the chicken, onions, ras el hanout, cinnamon and black pepper for about 10 minutes.

- Stir in the chickpeas, tomato puree, chicken cube and required amount of water that covers the mixture and cook, covered on medium heat for about 90 minutes.
- Meanwhile in a heatproof bowl, mix together pasta, 1/2 C. of water and a little bit of oil.
- Arrange the bowl in the steamer and steam for about 15 minutes.
- Remove from the steamer and use a little water to separate the pasta.
- In a pan of the water, hard boil the eggs and then peel and half them.
- In another large pan, add the pasta and gradually, add sauce from chicken mixture and cook till the pasta is done completely. (The mixture should be moist)
- Transfer the pasta into the serving platter.
- Top with the chicken pieces, followed by egg halves and remaining pan sauce.
- Serve with the crusty bread and green salad.

Amount per serving: 6

Timing Information:

| Preparation | 15 mins |
| Total Time | 1 hr 45 mins |

Nutritional Information:

Calories	918.7
Fat	43.7g
Cholesterol	279.3mg
Sodium	473.8mg
Carbohydrates	73.5g
Protein	54.1g

* Percent Daily Values are based on a 2,000 calorie diet.

Semolina & Seeds Bread

Ingredients

- 3 1/2 C. fine semolina
- 1 1/4 C. strong white bread flour
- 2 C. water, room temp. plus extra
- 4 fluid oz. sunflower oil
- 7 g fast action yeast
- 1 large egg, beaten
- 2 tsps sugar
- 2 tsps salt
- 2 large egg yolks, beaten
- 2 -3 tbsps sesame seeds
- 1 tbsp nigella seeds

Directions

- Grease a large round metal pan.
- In a larger bowl, mix together the flour, semolina, sugar, yeast and salt.
- With your hand, make a well in the center.
- Add the oil, egg and required amount of water and mix till a soft dough forms.
- With your hands, knead the dough for about 30 minutes, adding more water occasionally if required.

- Fold in the nigella seeds and with wet hands shape the dough into a ball.
- Transfer the dough into prepared pan, pressing gently downwards.
- Place some extra semolina on top evenly and keep aside, covered with the kitchen towel till rises to double in size.
- Set your oven to 355 degrees F and arrange the rack in the upper 1/3 of the oven.
- Coat the top of the dough with the beaten egg yolks and top with sesame seeds evenly.
- With a skewer, make 1 hole in the center of the dough and 5 about 1-inch from the edges.
- Cook in the oven for about 35 minutes.
- Remove from the oven and let it cool for about 5 minutes before removing from the pan.

Amount per serving: 1

Timing Information:

Preparation	2 hrs
Total Time	2 hrs 35 mins

Nutritional Information:

Calories	18656.0
Fat	1800.5g
Cholesterol	554.9mg
Sodium	4767.1mg
Carbohydrates	562.0g
Protein	107.9g

* Percent Daily Values are based on a 2,000 calorie diet.

Sweet Mini Treat

Ingredients

- 4 C. ground almonds
- 1 1/4 C. sugar
- 1 tbsp butter
- 1/2 tsp orange blossom water (mazhar)

- 3 tbsps corn flour, for dusting
- food coloring, of choice

For Decoration

- 3 tbsps sugar, for rolling
- glace cherries

Directions

- In a food processor, add the sugar, almonds, butter and mazhar and pulse till a firm paste forms.
- Divide the paste in 3 portions.
- In a bowl, add 2 portions of the paste and food coloring and mix well.
- Dust a smooth surface with the corn flour.
- Roll all three portions on a floured surface into a sausage shape.
- Cut the sausages into diamond shaped little pieces.
- Press 1 cherry in the center of each diamond and serve in tiny sweet cases.

Amount per serving: 1

Timing Information:

Preparation	1 hr
Total Time	1 hr

Nutritional Information:

Calories	87.0
Fat	5.0g
Cholesterol	0.7mg
Sodium	2.7mg
Carbohydrates	9.6g
Protein	2.0g

* Percent Daily Values are based on a 2,000 calorie diet.

Fluffy Egg & Semolina Pancake

Ingredients

- 6 eggs
- 1/2 tsp salt
- 4 -5 tsps vanilla flavoring
- 5 tbsps self raising flour
- 2 tbsps fine semolina
- 1 tsp baking powder
- To serve
- 1/4-1/2 C. honey

Directions

- In a large blender, add all the ingredients and pulse till a thick and bubbly mixture forms.
- Heat a greased skillet on low heat and add the mixture evenly.
- Cook for about 15 minutes and carefully change the side and cook for about 15 minutes more.
- Meanwhile warm the honey till melted slightly.
- Transfer the pancake into a serving platter and cut into equal sized wedges.
- Serve warm with a drizzling of the honey.

Amount per serving: 4

Timing Information:

Preparation	5 mins
Total Time	35 mins

Nutritional Information:

Calories	235.1
Fat	7.2g
Cholesterol	279.0mg
Sodium	489.2mg
Carbohydrates	29.3g
Protein	11.1g

* Percent Daily Values are based on a 2,000 calorie diet.

CHEESY POTATO & PICKLE ROLLS

Ingredients

- 20 -24 spring rolls, pastry sheets
- 2 1/2-3 C. mashed potatoes
- 3/4-1 C. cheddar cheese, grated
- 1/2 medium brown onion, finely chopped
- 1 medium pickled gherkin, finely chopped
- 3 tbsps fresh parsley, finely chopped
- 1 tbsp butter
- salt
- black pepper (freshly milled)
- flour, & water for the paste

Directions

- For filling, in a large bowl, mix together all the ingredients except spring roll sheets.
- Arrange the spring rolls onto a smooth surface.
- Divide the filling between the pastry rolls evenly, by placing in the center, leaving 1-inch space from all sides.
- Place the left side over the filling and then repeat with the right one.
- Now, place the bottom over the filling to cover it.

- With a pastry brush, coat the edges with the flour paste.
- Fold the rolls to secure the filling and fry the rolls in a little oil till golden brown from all sides.

Amount per serving: 1

Timing Information:

Preparation	25 mins
Total Time	50 mins

Nutritional Information:

Calories	68.5
Fat	2.2g
Cholesterol	5.6mg
Sodium	158.4mg
Carbohydrates	9.6g
Protein	2.3g

* Percent Daily Values are based on a 2,000 calorie diet.

Warm Veggie Salad

Ingredients

- 3 large green bell peppers
- 2 vine ripened tomatoes
- 1 -2 garlic clove, minced
- 2 -3 tbsps water
- 1 tsp olive oil
- salt
- vinegar, to taste

Directions

- Grill the peppers till softened and immediately place in a zip lock bag and keep aside for at least 5 minutes.
- Carefully peel the peppers and chop into 1 1/2-inch pieces.
- In a skillet, heat oil on medium heat and sauté the tomatoes, peppers and garlic for a few minutes.
- Stir in the salt, black pepper and water and cook, stirring occasionally for about 15 minutes.
- Serve with a drizzling of vinegar alongside crusty bread.

Amount per serving: 2

Timing Information:

Preparation	10 mins
Total Time	50 mins

Nutritional Information:

Calories	93.4
Fat	2.9g
Cholesterol	0.0mg
Sodium	14.1mg
Carbohydrates	16.7g
Protein	3.2g

* Percent Daily Values are based on a 2,000 calorie diet.

Veggie Stuffed Vine Leaves Rolls

Ingredients

- Stuffing Ingredients
- 50 grape leaves
- 1 large red pepper, chopped finely
- 1 large red vine-ripened tomatoes, chopped finely
- 1/2 large onion, chopped finely
- 4 garlic cloves, minced
- 1 1/2 C. basmati rice
- 1 tsp paprika
- 1/2 tsp cinnamon
- 1/2 tsp ras el hanout spice mix
- salt and black pepper
- 1 tbsp olive oil
- 4 tbsps water
- salt and black pepper
- Sauce Ingredients
- 1/2 large onion
- 1 large vine-ripened tomatoes
- 2 garlic cloves, minced
- 1/2 tsp cinnamon
- 1 chicken stock cube
- 1 liter water
- 1 tsp lemon juice

Directions

- For the preparation of fresh vine leaves, wash them and then trim the stalks.
- In lightly salted boiling water, blanch the leaves for about 15 minutes.
- Rinse the leaves then drain well and keep aside.

- For filling, in a large skillet, heat a little oil and stir fry the pepper, onion, tomatoes and garlic for about 4 minutes.
- Stir in the all spices and cook for about 30 seconds.
- Remove from heat and immediately, stir in rice, water and olive oil and keep aside.
- Arrange the leaves onto a smooth surface.
- Pace about the 1 tsp of the filling mixture in the bottom center of each leaf.
- First, fold the left corner over filling and then the right one.
- Gently roll the leaf to secure the filling.
- In a larger pan, place the rolls in 2-3 layers.
- Place a large heatproof plate over the rolls.
- In a bowl, mix together all the sauce ingredients and then place it over the rolls evenly.
- Cook, covered on medium heat for about 25 minutes.
- Serve these rolls with a drizzling of lemon juice.

Amount per serving: 1

Timing Information:

Preparation	50 mins
Total Time	1 hr 35 mins

Nutritional Information:

Calories	30.0
Fat	0.5g
Cholesterol	0.0mg
Sodium	138.5mg
Carbohydrates	5.7g
Protein	0.7g

* Percent Daily Values are based on a 2,000 calorie diet.

SPICY ROASTED CHICKEN

Ingredients

- 1 chicken
- 1 lemon
- 2 garlic cloves, crushed
- 1 bunch thyme
- 2 tbsps butter
- 1/2 tbsp ground cumin
- 1/2 tbsp ground coriander

Directions

- Set your oven to 375 degrees F before doing anything else.
- In a bowl, mix together the garlic, butter, spices and salt.
- With your fingers, loosen the skin under the breast and thighs.
- With your fingers rub the butter mixture under the skin and over the skin evenly and drizzle with lemon juice.
- Stuff the cavity of the chicken with thyme bunch and lemon halves.
- Sprinkle the chicken with the salt and black pepper generously.
- Arrange the chicken into prepared roasting pan, breast side down.
- Cook in the oven for about 80-90 minutes.

Amount per serving: 4

Timing Information:

Preparation	5 mins
Total Time	1 hr 25 mins

Nutritional Information:

Calories	305.9
Fat	23.1g
Cholesterol	100.3mg
Sodium	132.1mg
Carbohydrates	2.5g
Protein	21.6g

* Percent Daily Values are based on a 2,000 calorie diet.

Noodles with Chicken & Veggie Sauce

Ingredients

- 500 g plain flour
- 1/2 tsp salt
- water
- cornflour, to aid rolling out
- 1 tbsp ghee
- 1 1/2 kg chicken pieces
- 2 onions, finely chopped
- 1 garlic clove, minced
- 1 tbsp sunflower oil
- 1 C. of tinned chickpeas
- 1/4 tsp black pepper
- 2 1/4 tsps ras el hanout spice mix
- 1 liter water
- 1 tsp cinnamon
- 500 g long turnips, cut into 6ths
- 250 g potatoes, quartered
- 250 g courgettes, cut into 6ths
- 1 1/2 tsps salt

Directions

- In a large bowl, sift together the flour and salt.
- With your hands, make a well in the center.
- Slowly, add the water, mixing till a soft dough forms.
- Dust a smooth surface with the corn flour.
- Divide the dough into 4 portions and roll onto the floured surface into 1-2 mm thickness.
- With a little corn flour, dust the dough sheets and process in the pasta machine on the lowest settings.

- Keep aside the pasta sheets for about 20-30 minutes.
- Now, set the pasta machine to the settings that will cut the sheets into fine ribbons.
- Again with a little corn flour, dust the pasta sheets and process in the pasta machine to have the fine ribbons.
- Keep the noodles aside for at least 10 minutes.
- With a little oil, gently coat the noodles and cook in the steamer for about 5 minutes.
- Remove from steamer and drizzle with a little water to separate the noodles and steam for 5 minutes more.
- Transfer the noodles in a large dish and mix with the ghee and a little salt.
- For sauce in a large pan, heat the oil on medium heat and stir fry the chicken, onion, garlic and spices for about 10 minutes.
- Stir in the vegetables, seasoning and water and cook, covered for about 40 minutes.
- Stir in the chickpeas and cook, covered for about 20 minutes more.
- Transfer the noodles into the serving plates and top with the chicken mixture and serve.

Amount per serving: 8

Timing Information:

Preparation	45 mins
Total Time	1 hr 45 mins

Nutritional Information:

Calories	811.6
Fat	32.8g
Cholesterol	144.7mg
Sodium	855.1mg
Carbohydrates	79.8g
Protein	46.3g

* Percent Daily Values are based on a 2,000 calorie diet.

Veggies with Eggs

Ingredients

- 2 roma tomatoes, diced
- 1/2 C. , frozen tri-colored bell pepper strips thawed
- 2 tbsps extra virgin olive oil
- 1/2 C. onion, sliced thinly
- 1 medium garlic clove, minced
- 1 tsp paprika
- 1/2 tbsp of cold unsalted butter
- 3/4 tsp kosher salt, to taste
- 1 tsp fresh black pepper
- 4 large eggs, room temperature
- 2 tsps flat-leaf Italian parsley, chopped

Directions

- In a large bowl, add the peppers, tomatoes, 1 tbsp of the oil, salt and black pepper and toss to coat.
- In another bowl, mix together the onions, garlic, remaining oil, paprika, salt and black pepper and toss to coat.
- In a 9-inch round cake pan, place the peppers mixture on one side and the onion mixture on the other side.

- Place the butter on top of both mixtures.
- Arrange the pan into a slow cooker and slow cook for about 2 hours.
- With a spatula, stir all the ingredients in the pan till well combined and slowly cook for about 1 hour more.
- With a wooden spoon, make 4 wells in the vegetable mixture.
- Crack the eggs, one at a time in a small bowl and sprinkle with salt and black pepper.
- Carefully, place 1 egg in each well and slow cook for about 25-30 minutes more.
- Serve with a garnishing of parsley alongside the rice or bread.

Amount per serving: 4

Timing Information:

Preparation	10 mins
Total Time	3 hrs 10 mins

Nutritional Information:

Calories	164.4
Fat	13.3g
Cholesterol	215.3mg
Sodium	401.0mg
Carbohydrates	4.6g
Protein	6.9g

* Percent Daily Values are based on a 2,000 calorie diet.

CHICKEN & CHICKPEAS WITH FRENCH FRIES

Ingredients

- 2 tbsps oil
- 1/2 C. onion, chopped
- 1 lb skinless chicken piece, rid of fat and skin
- 10 sprigs flat leaf parsley, leaves only, chopped
- 1/4 C. chickpeas, cooked
- 1 tsp black pepper
- 1 tsp salt
- 1/2 tsp cinnamon
- 3 C. water
- 2 lbs frozen french fries
- 1 egg, beaten
- lemon wedge, for serving

Directions

- In a pan, heat the oil on low heat and stir in the chicken, chickpeas, onion, half of the parsley, cinnamon and salt.
- Cover and simmer, stirring occasionally for about 10 minutes.
- Stir in the water and bring to a boil on medium heat.
- Cook for about 40 minutes.

- Meanwhile, cook the French fries according to package's instructions.
- Stir in the beaten egg and French fries in the pan and simmer for about 10 minutes more.
- Serve with a garnishing of the remaining parsley.

Amount per serving: 6

Timing Information:

Preparation	20 mins
Total Time	1 hr 10 mins

Nutritional Information:

Calories	332.8
Fat	13.5g
Cholesterol	53.9mg
Sodium	962.1mg
Carbohydrates	41.6g
Protein	12.2g

* Percent Daily Values are based on a 2,000 calorie diet.

ARABIC STYLE LAMB WITH SAUCE

Ingredients

- 800 g fresh lamb liver
- 6 -8 garlic cloves, minced
- 2 C. chopped tinned tomatoes with juice
- 1/2 C. chopped fresh coriander
- 2 -3 tsps fresh ground cumin
- salt & freshly ground black pepper
- 1 C. water
- 2 tbsps good quality olive oil

Directions

- Cut the lamb liver into 1-inch long and 1/2-inch wide pieces.
- In large frying pan, heat the oil on medium heat and stir fry the liver till browned from all sides.
- Increase the heat to medium-high and sauté the garlic and cumin for a while.
- Meanwhile in a blender, pulse the tomatoes with juice till a fine puree forms.
- In the pan, stir in tomato puree, water, salt and black pepper and cook, covered for about 25 minutes.
- Stir in half of the coriander and remove from heat.

- Serve with a garnishing of the remaining coriander alongside your desired side dish.

Amount per serving: 4

Timing Information:

Preparation	15 mins
Total Time	50 mins

Nutritional Information:

Calories	382.7
Fat	17.2g
Cholesterol	741.9mg
Sodium	427.9mg
Carbohydrates	13.8g
Protein	42.3g

* Percent Daily Values are based on a 2,000 calorie diet.

ALMOND BAKLAWA

Ingredients

- 24 oz. plain flour
- 310 ml water
- 200 ml melted ghee mixed with 110ml sunflower oil
- 1/2 tsp salt
- 18 oz. chopped almonds
- 128 g granulated sugar
- 1/4 tsp ground cinnamon
- 1 tsp vanilla sugar
- 2 tsps melted ghee
- 155 ml orange flower water (mazhar)
- 310 -620 ml honey
- 155 -310 ml orange flower water (mazhar)
- 310 ml extra of melted ghee

Directions

- Set your oven to 300 degrees F before doing anything else and grease a large tray with a little melted ghee.
- In a bowl, mix together the flour, salt and ghee/oil mixture.
- Slowly, add the water and mix till a smooth dough forms.
- Dust a smooth surface with the corn flour.
- Divide the dough into 2 portions and place one onto floured surface, covered with a kitchen towel.
- Shape another portion into golf sized balls.
- Roll the balls into sausage shapes and again roll on a floured surface into a 3-4 mm thickness.

- With a little corn flour, dust the dough sheets and process in the pasta machine on the lowest settings for thinnest strips.
- Arrange the first strip vertically in the center of prepared tray and coat with ghee.
- Place a second strip horizontally over the first strip.
- Repeat with the remaining strips and ghee, covering the tray completely in 5 layers. (There should be 5 strips in each layer)
- For filling in a food processor, add the almonds and pulse till chopped finely.
- Transfer the almonds into a bowl with the sugar, vanilla sugar, cinnamon and mazhar and mix till well combined.
- Place the filling over strips evenly in the tray and with a spatula, smooth the surface gently.
- Roll the other dough portion and make golf size balls.
- Roll the ball into sausage shape and again roll onto floured surface into 3-4 mm thickness.
- With a little corn flour, dust the dough sheets and process in the pasta machine on the lowest settings for thinnest strips.
- Place the strips over filling in the same process you have for the first portion. (This time you should have 6 layers of strips)
- With a knife, cut the straight vertical lines all the way to bottom and then cut more lines diagonally to make diamond shape.
- Press a whole almond in the center of each diamond.
- Cook in the oven for about 60-70 minutes.
- For syrup in a pan, warm the mazhar and honey.
- Remove the baking tray from the oven and pour the syrup over the baklawa and keep aside for at least 10 minutes.
- Cut into desired pieces and serve.

Amount per serving: 20

Timing Information:

Preparation	1 hr
Total Time	2 hrs 10 mins

Nutritional Information:

Calories	545.7
Fat	36.0g
Cholesterol	35.6mg
Sodium	231.2mg
Carbohydrates	51.3g
Protein	8.0g

* Percent Daily Values are based on a 2,000 calorie diet.

SEMOLINA FLATBREAD

Ingredients

- 2 C. semolina flour
- 1 tbsp salt
- 1/4 C. olive oil
- 1 C. water

Directions

- In a bowl, mix together all the ingredients except water.
- Slowly, add the water and mix till a soft dough forms.
- Make 2 equal sized balls from dough and flatten onto lightly floured surface to your desired size.
- Heat a frying pan on medium heat and cook from both sides till golden brown.
- Cut into desired size wedges before serving.

Amount per serving: 8

Timing Information:

Preparation	10 mins
Total Time	25 mins

Nutritional Information:

Calories	209.9
Fat	7.1g
Cholesterol	0.0mg
Sodium	873.5mg
Carbohydrates	30.4g
Protein	5.2g

* Percent Daily Values are based on a 2,000 calorie diet.

Fish & Veggie Soup

Ingredients

- 1 kg fish fillet
- 2 large potatoes
- 2 green bell peppers
- 1 large carrot
- 1 fennel bulb
- 2 onions
- 1 celery rib
- 4 tbsps tomato paste
- 2 liters water
- 1 tbsp cumin
- 1 tsp ras el hanout spice mix
- 1 tsp coriander
- 2 bay leaves
- 1 piece lemon rind
- 1 tbsp harissa
- 4 tbsps olive oil

Directions

- Chop the onion and then sauté in heated oil till golden in a large soup pan.
- Chop all the vegetables and cook in the pan till soft.
- Stir in the tomato paste and cook for a few seconds.
- Add the water, lemon rind and spices and bring to a boil.
- Reduce the heat to low and simmer for about 20 minutes.
- Cut the fish into cubes and stir in the soup.
- Simmer for about 15 minutes more.
- With a hand blender, puree the soup to the desired consistency.
- Serve with the baguette bread and lemon slices.

Amount per serving: 6

Timing Information:

Preparation	15 mins
Total Time	55 mins

Nutritional Information:

Calories	402.5
Fat	11.0g
Cholesterol	91.6mg
Sodium	270.3mg
Carbohydrates	33.4g
Protein	42.5g

* Percent Daily Values are based on a 2,000 calorie diet.

SPICY EGGPLANT

Ingredients

- 2 eggplants
- 2 garlic cloves, crushed
- 1 tsp sweet paprika
- 1 1/2 tsps cumin, ground
- 1/2 tsp sugar
- 1 tbsp lemon juice

Directions

- Cut the eggplant into 1/2-inch slices and place in a colander.
- Sprinkle with salt and keep aside for about 20 minutes to drain.
- Rinse well and gently squeeze, then pat dry.
- In a large frying pan, heat about 1/4-inch of the oil on medium heat and fry the eggplant slices in batches till golden brown from both sides.
- Transfer the eggplant slices onto a paper towel lined plate to drain and then chop them finely.
- In a bowl, add the chopped eggplant slices with garlic, sugar, cumin and paprika.
- With a paper towel, wipe the frying pan and place it on medium heat.
- Add the eggplant mixture and cook, stirring continuously for about 2 minutes.
- Serve with a drizzling of lemon juice.

Amount per serving: 6

Timing Information:

Preparation	10 mins
Total Time	30 mins

Nutritional Information:

Calories	43.0
Fat	0.4g
Cholesterol	0.0mg
Sodium	4.3mg
Carbohydrates	10.0g
Protein	1.7g

* Percent Daily Values are based on a 2,000 calorie diet.

Garbanzo Beans & Veggie Soup

Ingredients

- 1 onion
- 2 garlic cloves
- 2 tbsps cilantro
- 2 tbsps olive oil
- 2 carrots, cut into large pieces
- 1 large potato, cut into large pieces
- 1 1/2 C. butternut squash, cut into large pieces

- 2 tbsps tomato paste
- 1 C. garbanzo beans
- 2 tbsps bulgher wheat
- 8 C. water
- 1 tsp salt
- pepper, to taste
- 1 tsp paprika
- 1 pinch cayenne (optional)

Directions

- In a skillet, heat the oil and sauté onion and garlic till tender.
- Stir in the vegetables, cilantro and spices and then pour in water.
- Simmer, covered on medium heat for about 15 minutes.
- Transfer the vegetables into a large bowl and with a hand blender, mash them.
- In the same pan, add the mashed vegetables with beans, bulgur wheat and tomato paste and simmer for about 10-15 minutes more.

Amount per serving: 1

Timing Information:

Preparation	20 mins
Total Time	55 mins

Nutritional Information:

Calories	138.6
Fat	3.9g
Cholesterol	0.0mg
Sodium	434.6mg
Carbohydrates	23.7g
Protein	3.5g

* Percent Daily Values are based on a 2,000 calorie diet.

ALMOND BREAD WITH ORANGE BLOSSOM SYRUP

Ingredients

- 1 C. egg
- 1 C. sugar
- 1 C. butter
- 1 C. of freshly ground almonds
- 1 C. stale bread
- 1 1/2 tsps baking powder
- 1 lemon, zest of, large
- 1/2 tsp vanilla essence

For the Syrup

- 2 C. granulated sugar
- 4 C. water
- 1 1/2 tbsps orange blossom water (mazhar)

Directions

- Set your oven to 375 degrees F before doing anything else.
- For Syrup, in a pan, mix together the water and sugar and boil for about 10-15 minutes.
- Stir in the mazhar in the last couple of minutes.
- Remove from heat and let it cool slightly.
- In a bowl, crack the eggs and beat till fluffy.
- Add butter and sugar and beat till well combined and then fold in remaining ingredients.

- Transfer the mixture into a round metal tin and with the back of a spatula, smooth the surface.
- Cook in the oven for about 40 minutes or till a toothpick inserted in the center comes out clean.
- Remove from the oven and pour the sugar syrup over bread.
- Cut the bread into desired slices and serve.

Amount per serving: 15

Timing Information:

Preparation	20 mins
Total Time	1 hr 15 mins

Nutritional Information:

Calories	348.8
Fat	18.8g
Cholesterol	101.0mg
Sodium	194.5mg
Carbohydrates	43.2g
Protein	4.3g

* Percent Daily Values are based on a 2,000 calorie diet.

Spicy Lamb Sausage

Ingredients

- 2 lbs boneless lamb, cut into 2 inch pieces
- 4 oz. lamb fat attached to the lamb kidney
- 2 heads garlic, about 12 cloves, peeled
- 1 tsp salt (to taste)
- 1 tsp black pepper
- 1 tbsp ground cumin
- 1 tbsp ground coriander
- 1 tbsp sumac
- 1 tbsp red hot chili powder
- 2 tbsps sweet paprika
- 1 C. cold water
- 1 small lamb intestine casing

Directions

- In a grinder, add the lamb, fat from lamb kidneys, and garlic and grind well.
- Add the remaining ingredients except casing and grind till well combined.
- Make mini patties from the mixture and fry each patty in a little oil.
- Tightly, tie the one side of the casing.

- In the casing add the lamb mixture and twist after every 4-inches to divide into individual sausages.
- Fry these sausages in vegetable oil till golden brown.

Amount per serving: 1

Timing Information:

Preparation	35 mins
Total Time	35 mins

Nutritional Information:

Calories	306.9
Fat	22.5g
Cholesterol	78.1mg
Sodium	306.6mg
Carbohydrates	5.8g
Protein	19.9g

* Percent Daily Values are based on a 2,000 calorie diet.

SEMOLINA PANCAKES

Ingredients

- 2 C. fine semolina
- 1 C. plain flour
- 1 C. whole wheat flour
- 3 eggs
- 2 tsps baking powder
- 1 tbsp instant yeast
- 2 tsps sugar
- 1 pinch salt
- 1 C. warm water
- 2 C. milk
- 1 tbsp vegetable oil (optional)

Directions

- In a large bowl, mix together the flours, semolina, eggs, yeast, sugar, baking powder and salt.
- Slowly, add the milk and water and mix till a thick but runny mixture forms.
- In a frying pan, heat a little oil and add the desired amount of the mixture and tilt the pan to coat the bottom.
- Cook on both sides till desired doneness.

Amount per serving: 6

Timing Information:

Preparation	10 mins
Total Time	40 mins

Nutritional Information:

Calories	444.7
Fat	6.8g
Cholesterol	104.3mg
Sodium	225.8mg
Carbohydrates	77.3g
Protein	18.4g

* Percent Daily Values are based on a 2,000 calorie diet.

SPICED FLATBREAD

Ingredients

- 3 C. finely ground whole wheat flour
- 1 tsp salt
- 1/2 C. olive oil, divided
- 1 1/2 C. water
- 1 tsp ground cumin
- 1 tsp sweet paprika
- 1 tsp turmeric

Directions

- For dough in a large bowl, mix together 2 tbsps of the oil, flour and salt.
- Slowly, add the required amount of the water and mix till a soft dough forms.
- Place the dough onto a floured surface and knead for about 15 minutes. (Dust with a little flour while kneading)
- Make a ball from the dough and brush with 2 tbsps of oil.
- Place the dough ball in a bowl and with a plastic wrap, cover the bowl.
- Keep aside in the warm place for about 1 hour.
- In a small bowl, mix together the remaining 1/4 C. of oil and spices.
- For the flatbread divide the dough into 12 equal sized balls and flatten the each ball into a disk.

- Place the disks, one at a time onto a lightly floured surface and with a rolling pin, roll the each disk thinly into a 9-inch round.
- With your fingertips, spread about 1 tsp of spiced oil over each flat bread and tightly roll up into a long cylinder and then coil into a tight spiral.
- Place one flatbread onto a large parchment paper and cover with plastic wrap.
- Place the remaining flatbreads in the same way.
- Arrange a parchment paper onto a smooth surface and roll each spiral into 6-inches round.
- Heat a large cast-iron skillet on medium heat and cook each flatbread for about 3-4 minutes, turning once.

Amount per serving: 1

Timing Information:

Preparation	50 mins
Total Time	54 mins

Nutritional Information:

Calories	183.4
Fat	9.8g
Cholesterol	0.0mg
Sodium	195.9mg
Carbohydrates	21.8g
Protein	4.0g

* Percent Daily Values are based on a 2,000 calorie diet.

Cauliflower in Spicy Sauce

Ingredients

- 8 oz. tomatoes, chopped
- 2 large garlic cloves, finely chopped
- 4 tbsps olive oil
- 1 tsp paprika
- 1 tsp salt
- 1 tsp black pepper
- 1 tsp harissa
- 1 cauliflower, medium sized, trimmed, cut into florets

Directions

- In a pan of salted water, cook the cauliflower for about 7-8 minutes.
- Drain the cauliflower well, reserving some cooking liquid.
- Meanwhile in another pan, heat the oil and sauté the garlic for about 1 minute.
- Stir in the remaining ingredients and reduce the heat to low.
- Simmer the sauce for about 10 minutes and stir in the cauliflower.
- Simmer, stirring occasionally for about 5 minutes. (Use reserved water if sauce is to thick)
- Serve this dish over boiled rice with a garnishing of parsley.

Amount per serving: 4

Timing Information:

Preparation	5 mins
Total Time	25 mins

Nutritional Information:

Calories	171.1
Fat	13.8g
Cholesterol	0.0mg
Sodium	628.3mg
Carbohydrates	11.0g
Protein	3.6g

* Percent Daily Values are based on a 2,000 calorie diet.

DRIED FRUIT BALLS

Ingredients

- 1 3/4 C. pitted prunes, chopped
- 1 3/4 C. dried figs
- 1/4 C. sweet red wine
- 1 tsp cinnamon
- 1/4 tsp nutmeg
- 2 tbsps confectioners' sugar

Directions

- In a large food processor, add all the ingredients and pulse till a smooth mixture forms.
- Roll into walnut sized balls and serve. (For better result you can mix in 1 C. of almonds)

Amount per serving: 1

Timing Information:

Preparation	5 mins
Total Time	5 mins

Nutritional Information:

Calories	192.7
Fat	0.6g
Cholesterol	0.0mg
Sodium	7.2mg
Carbohydrates	46.6g
Protein	2.2g

* Percent Daily Values are based on a 2,000 calorie diet.

PEPPERS FILLED PASTRIES

Ingredients

- 4 onions
- 2 tbsps concentrated tomato puree
- 2 green peppers
- 2 tbsps olive oil
- salt & pepper
- 1 hot pepper
- 500 g fine semolina
- 250 g plain flour
- salt
- water

Directions

- For filling, core the peppers and cut into fine strips and then cut the onions into rings.
- In a skillet, heat a little oil and sauté the peppers and onions till softened.
- Stir in the tomato puree, salt and black pepper and simmer, covered for about 5 minutes.
- Remove from heat and let it cool.
- For pastry, in a bowl mix the semolina, flour and salt.

- With your hands, make a well in the center of the mixture.
- Slowly, add the required amount of water and knead for about 8-10 minutes till a stiff dough forms.
- Divide the dough and then roll into golf sized balls.
- Place the balls, one at a time onto a greased surface and stretch out thinly.
- Divide the filling mixture in the center of each pastry and fold all the edges, one at a time to form a square parcel.
- In a large skillet, heat the oil and fry the parcels till golden brown from both sides.

Amount per serving: 10

Timing Information:

Preparation	40 mins
Total Time	1 hr

Nutritional Information:

Calories	342.0
Fat	3.6g
Cholesterol	0.0mg
Sodium	4.0mg
Carbohydrates	66.1g
Protein	10.2g

* Percent Daily Values are based on a 2,000 calorie diet.

THANKS FOR READING! NOW LET'S TRY SOME **SAMOSAS**, **BIRYANI**, AND **MOROCCAN** ....

 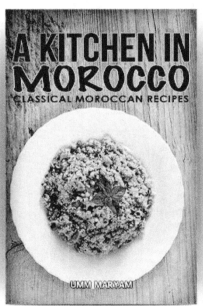 

http://bit.ly/1R3gfGh

To grab this **box set** simply follow the link mentioned above, or tap the book cover.

This will take you to a page where you can simply enter your email address and a PDF version of **the box set** will be emailed to you.

I hope you are ready for some serious **cultural cooking**!

http://bit.ly/1R3gfGh

You will also receive updates on my new books, and various musings about food and cultural cooking.

Also don't forget to like and subscribe on the social networks. I love meeting my readers. Links to all my profiles are below so please click and connect :)

Facebook

Twitter

Google +

Come On...
Let's Be Friends :)

I adore my readers and love connecting with them socially. Please follow the links below so we can connect on Facebook, Twitter, and Google+.

Facebook

Twitter

Google +

I also have a blog that I regularly update for my readers so check it out below.

My Blog

CAN I ASK A FAVOUR?

If you found this book interesting, or have otherwise found any benefit in it. Then may I ask that you post a review of it on Amazon? Nothing excites me more than new reviews, especially reviews which suggest new topics for writing. I do read all reviews and I always factor feedback into my newer works.

So if you are willing to take ten minutes to write what you sincerely thought about this book then please visit our Amazon page and post your opinions.

Again thank you!

INTERESTED IN MY OTHER COOKBOOKS?

For more great cookbooks check out my Amazon Author page:

For a complete listing of all my books please see my author page.

Printed in Great Britain
by Amazon

26860347R00079